IMAGES
of America

THE OKLAHOMA
PANHANDLE

IMAGES
of America

THE OKLAHOMA PANHANDLE

Sara Jane Richter

ARCADIA
PUBLISHING

Published by Arcadia Publishing
Charleston, South Carolina

Library of Congress Control Number: 2011928808

For all general information, please contact Arcadia Publishing:
Telephone 843-853-2070
Fax 843-853-0044
E-mail sales@arcadiapublishing.com
For customer service and orders:
Toll-Free 1-888-313-2665

Visit us on the Internet at www.arcadiapublishing.com

*This book is dedicated to seven special people:
my brother and sister-in-law, Kevin and Debbie, who give
me unflagging love, support, and encouragement;
my mother and father, Pauline and Russel, who told me that I
could do anything and would love me even if I might fail;
my friends, Troy and Tito, who share meals,
laughter, travel, and conversation;
my friend, Tom, with whom I first investigated and wrote
about our adopted home—the Oklahoma Panhandle.*

CONTENTS

ACKNOWLEDGMENTS

Few tasks are accomplished by single individuals, and the creation of this volume is no exception. I must thank those who encouraged and helped me with this project, such as those from Beaver County: Dr. Harold and Joan Kachel, Dr. V. Pauline Hodges, and Julie O'Reilly of the Jones-Plummer Trail Museum; in Texas County, Debbie Colson and Sue Weissinger of the No Man's Land Museum and Virginia Roach of the Texhoma Historical Society shared photographs and history; help in Cimarron County came from Phyllis Randolph of the Cimarron Heritage Center. Tito Aznar graciously contributed his photography skills, technical expertise, and friendship. Laura Hays lent her expert proofreading eye. I appreciate all who generously shared photographs. Louie, too, gave me constant "purring" support and reasons to smile as I worked on the text. Lastly, I must extend my appreciation to my employer, Oklahoma Panhandle State University, for allowing me the time and indulgence to work on this project.

I have lived in the Oklahoma Panhandle since 1985, and I couldn't think of anywhere else I'd really like to live. The remote, lonesome, and often overlooked 'handle has a mystique and history unique to Oklahoma. I like it and am proud to call it my home.

Photographs without credit given come from the author's personal collection.

INTRODUCTION

Most folks share a fundamental desire to own some land. Humans have an intrinsic need to rub soil between their hands, to know that it is their dirt and that they own it. The western hemisphere was "discovered" so that a new trading route might be had. Manifest destiny held that Americans deserved the entire western hemisphere. Much of the western United States, including Oklahoma, was settled and tamed based on an American dream: the belief that if people owned 160 acres, they could create paradise, support themselves and a family, and live like royalty—that old Jeffersonian ideal. The federal government promoted such mythology with legislative actions such as the Homestead Act, land giveaways, and federal land runs, such as the one in Oklahoma Territory in 1889. The University of Oklahoma named its mascot for the eager land seekers led by David L. Payne, who broke the law to get a piece of unclaimed land *sooner* than the government had allowed. Indeed, many people have died for the privilege of owning land. Wars have been fought over turf, even little pieces of real estate.

However, the Oklahoma Panhandle flies in the face of such interest and determination to possess hallowed ground. The Panhandle is land no one wanted, and its nicknames—"No Man's Land," "the Neutral Strip," and "the Public Lands"—reflect this. Several nations have claimed this area, measuring 166.8 miles by 34.4 miles, including Spain, England, France, the United States, Mexico, and the Republic of Texas. Texas last gave up claim to the land when, in 1850, the United States purchased the strip of land for $10 million to absolve Texas of its indebtedness following the Mexican War. The government created this parcel, which is still in its original shape, due to political reasons. The Kansas-Nebraska Act prohibited slavery below the 36th parallel, yet Texas was a slave state, so it shed territory north of that line, creating the southern border of No Man's Land. Kansas set its southern boundary at the 37th parallel, so the top of the Neutral Strip was set in 1861. The eastern boundary came in 1803 with the Louisiana Purchase, while the formation of the Arizona Territory in 1863 established the western border. After its dimensions were established, the Neutral Strip became a geographic football, kicked around for years with no one to claim it. The fact that no one wanted this real estate for so long contributes to the pride and independence that Panhandle residents feel about living somewhere that no one really wanted.

No state or territory wanted, asked for, or even connived for it—not Colorado, Kansas, New Mexico, or Texas. A Beaver, Oklahoma, newspaper editor called No Man's Land an orphan. It possessed no real value except as grazing land. It certainly had no law because it did not lie within the boundaries of any judicial district. Therefore, it sat unwanted, unused, and unprotected for decades before the US government unilaterally attached it to Oklahoma Territory to "fill out" the state in 1890. Finally, the Neutral Strip might be governed. Until that time, it had no law, a small population, and not much of a future. However, it did have quite a history, a history usually involving individuals who moved around inside or across the region. There just has not been a host of folks who have opted to stay permanently in No Man's Land.

This piece of real estate possesses a certain charm that is only tangible to those who truly want a place to belong. Living in the 'handle is not for everyone. "Dust Bowl tough" describes the spirit of this place, and not everyone who has tried to live here has lived here long. Inhabitants must have a sense of humor and appreciate the area's many oddities. Far from malls, theatres, fine dining, airports, and cultural activities, the Oklahoma Panhandle does not appeal to the majority. However, those who seek wide-open spaces, clean air, and independence will find the Oklahoma Panhandle just right. Shhhh . . . the Panhandle is the best-kept secret in the state of Oklahoma.

One

WONDERS OF
THE PANHANDLE

The Oklahoma Panhandle has many unique elements—landscapes, history, and annual events. Here, the western edge of the short grass prairie meets the eastern edge of the Rocky Mountains. The Panhandle has been called the "geological wonder of the North American continent." Indeed, the geology of the region is fascinating. The highest elevation in the state of Oklahoma rises in the far northwestern corner of the Panhandle in the Black Mesa area, where Mother Nature has been artistic with water, wind, and rain to craft some unusual looking rocks. The Panhandle once served as a beach for the ancient eastern and western seas that covered much of North America millions of years ago. Nowhere else in the state can geologists study exposed Jurassic, Triassic, Carnian, and Norian rocks some 134 million to 230 million years old. Such formations occur only in two other places in the country: Dinosaur Ridge near Denver, Colorado, and Dinosaur National Monument near Vernal, Utah. Dinosaurs roamed the Panhandle, as evidenced in their fossilized footprints and excavated bones. Because of this rare geology, the Panhandle sits in the midst of the Hugoton Gas Field, one of the richest deposits of natural gas in the United States.

Historians have much to study in the Panhandle as well, including ancient peoples, commercial trails, and Native Americans. Not many people have stayed in the Oklahoma Panhandle, but many have travelled through it. Panhandlers honor their unique heritage with celebrations such as Pioneer Days, Santa Fe Trail Daze, and cow-chip throwing contests.

When outsiders come to the 'handle, they are amazed by what they see and have the opportunity to experience and often cannot believe that they have waited so long to come to the Panhandle. Even people who have lived here for years can discover something new every day about their home turf. For a space so small, it is full of amazing things.

This series of footprints was made by an allosaurus millions of years ago in what is today Cooper's Canyon in northwestern Cimarron County. It is one of many traces of prehistoric times in the Black Mesa area. As late as the 1970s, visitors could see at least 40 prints at this location, but Mother Nature has erased them over time. The single small dinosaur print was taken at a rocky ridge overlooking Lake Carl G. Etling in Cimarron County. Many similar prints dot the location just off the winding road that snakes its way through Black Mesa State Park. (At left, courtesy Charla Lewis; below, Tito Aznar.)

From this Cimarron County location, archeologists excavated hundreds of dinosaur bones. On the upper left is a plaster cast of the first bone found here. In 1931, while grading a dirt road (now State Highway 325), Pard Collins of Kenton unearthed what he thought was a big rock. He called his friend Tucker Truman to investigate, and together, they uncovered the leg bone of a prehistoric beast. That bone was nearly six feet long and weighed over 400 pounds. A total of eight dinosaur quarry locations have been established in the county, and with federal and state monies through the years, scientists have removed over 6,000 bones weighing more than 18 tons. From 1935 until 1942, J. Willis Stovall, from the University of Oklahoma, directed a Works Project Administration (WPA) endeavor to excavate bones from 17 sites in the Black Mesa area. A nearly complete 70-foot brontosaurus skeleton, now displayed at the Sam Noble Oklahoma Museum of Natural History in Norman, came from Cimarron County. (Courtesy Tito Aznar.)

"Cimmy," an 18,000-pound, handcrafted, life-sized iron apatosaurus dinosaur, stands on the north side of the grounds of the Cimarron Heritage Center in Boise City. Joe Barrington of Throckmorton, Texas, constructed Cimmy with funds donated by Bob and Norma Gene Young. The structure stands 35 feet tall and is 65 feet long. Cimarron County takes great pride in its dinosaur legacy and uses it as a tourist draw. There are even bumper stickers cautioning onlookers to beware because drivers "brake for dinosaurs."

In 1964, the No Man's Land Historical Society sponsored a dig to retrieve a mastodon fossil. Faculty and students in the Panhandle Agricultural and Mechanical College Museum Club did the actual digging in Beaver County under the direction of faculty members Dr. Harold S. Kachel and Dr. Harold M. Hefley. Some of the bones are housed in the collections of the No Man's Land Museum in Goodwell, Oklahoma. (Courtesy Harold S. Kachel and Harold M. Hefley.)

This example of ogham (also spelled "ogam"), the long notches incised on rock faces in far western and very remote Cimarron County, prove at least to some archeologists and historians that white men roamed the interior of North America long before Christopher Columbus crossed the Atlantic Ocean. Ogham, an ancient Celtic writing system, hasn't really been translated, but such markings have been found in the British Isles, Europe, and other places. It is thought that ogham originated as an accounting system and was used primarily to mark boundaries. Earliest known ogham inscriptions date from the 4th century ACE. (Courtesy Harold Kachel.)

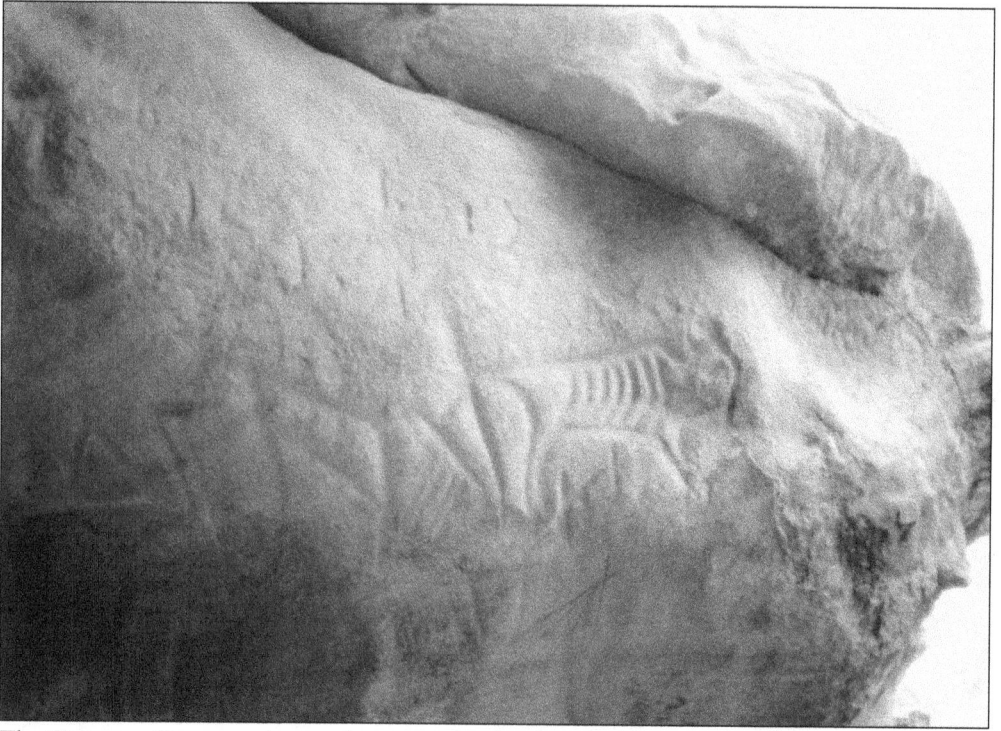

The Cimarron County rock seen above is in Anubis Cave and bears pictographs drawn by ancient native peoples. Near Folsom, New Mexico, the oldest human artifacts in the United States—Folsom points—were found in 1926 on the Crowfoot Ranch. Because of this, archeologists say that man inhabited North America 10,000 years ago. It stands to reason that those people wandered into the Panhandle. The Indian pictograph below is additional evidence of ancient peoples living in the Oklahoma Panhandle; however, these markings no longer exist. Through the years, cattle along the Cimarron River north of Goodwell in Texas County have rubbed them off the riverbank. (Both courtesy Harold Kachel.)

Excavation of this ancient Native American settlement near Guymon in Texas County occurred in 1972. Archeologists from the University of Oklahoma in Norman dug out the site, dated approximately 1300 ACE, retrieved artifacts, and then covered the site for preservation. In the late 1800s, a man from Chicago built two homes for his two homesteading daughters near this location, so it is known as the "Two Sisters" site. (Courtesy Harold Kachel.)

This archeological location is in Beaver County along Clear Creek and is known as the Yates site. It dates from 1340 and was apparently a community trading area for local and traveling native populations. Archeologists from the University of Oklahoma excavated the site and then closed it in the 1970s. (Courtesy Harold Kachel.)

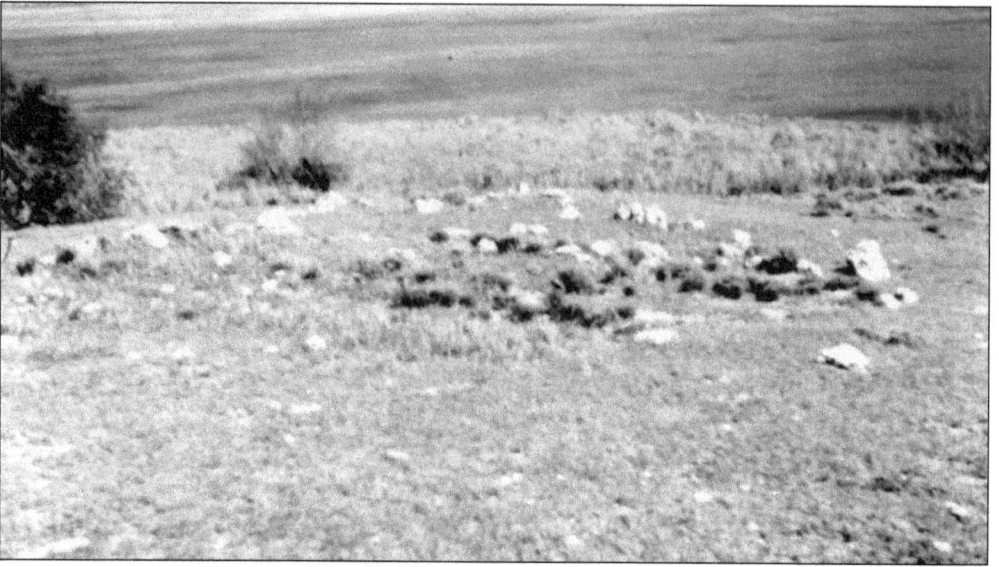

This teepee ring—a circle of rocks—near Optima in Texas County is a sign of Plains Indians who put rocks around the bottoms of teepees to keep them secure. Western Oklahoma, eastern New Mexico, and the Texas and Oklahoma Panhandles were nicknamed "Comancheria," as the Comanche held power until 1876. The Panhandle had few permanent Indian settlements, but Indians followed the buffalo herds' migrations through the region. (Courtesy Harold Kachel.)

Conservationists estimate that the Panhandle supported five million buffalo at a time. Of course, the animal was the mainstay of the Plains tribes' lifestyle. In the 1870s, white hunters killed bison for hides and tongues. The last buffalo herd lived in the Panhandle in the late 1880s, a piddling percentage of the number that lived before the white man came. The last wild buffalo in the Panhandle roamed along the Texas border south of Boise City in 1890. (Courtesy Charla Lewis.)

16

The Panhandle has belonged to at least five different nations: Spain, France, Mexico, Texas, and the United States. In addition, it was part of Comancheria during the height of the Comanche tribe's domination of the Southern Plains in the 1870s. The No Man's Land Museum in Goodwell, Texas County, displays these flags over the building's entrance. (Courtesy Tito Aznar.)

Francisco Vasquez de Coronado traveled through Beaver County searching for the Lost Cities of Gold. In his 1541 journals, Coronado lamented the terrain's lack of landmarks and compared walking in the endless grass to sailing on the sea. Guides got lost with no physical markers to guide them. In Cimarron County, one of Coronado's expedition teams perhaps carved "Coronatto 1541" on a rock, but its authenticity is not proven.

These are snow-filled ruts of the Cimarron Route of the Santa Fe Trail that angled southward near Dodge City, Kansas, and cut across 20 miles of northwest Cimarron County on its way to Santa Fe. The route is also known as the Jornado del Muerte, the "Journey of Death." The exact route of the trail is not known, but it was famous for its nonexistent water, dangerous Indians, and fierce weather.

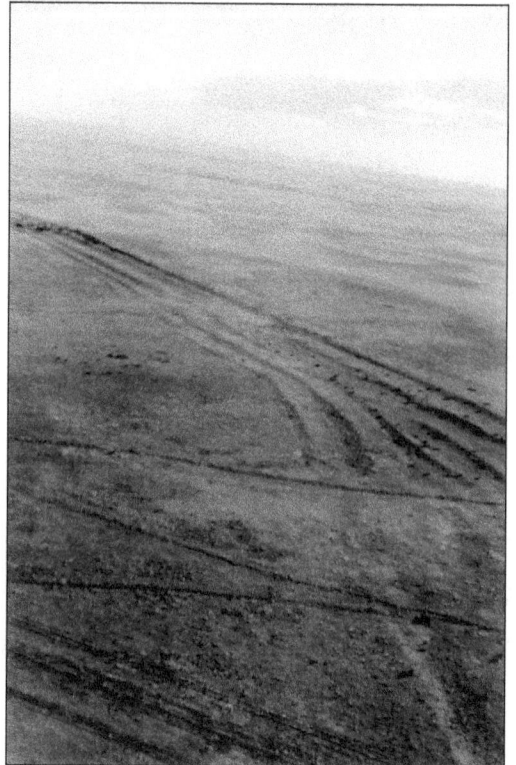

This aerial shot by Paul Smith shows many deep ruts of the Cimarron Route, which cut about 100 miles and 10 days off the trip from Independence, Missouri, to Santa Fe. If travelers opted to take the safer mountain route through southeast Colorado, the trip took approximately 75 days. (Courtesy Cimarron Heritage Center.)

Near Willow Bar, the Cimarron River enters the Panhandle. At this location, a blizzard surprised Albert Speyer and killed his animals, so he and his men walked to Dodge City, Kansas, purchased animals, drove them back, and carried on to Santa Fe. For years, traders would spell out words and draw pictures with the bones for entertainment. (Courtesy Cimarron Heritage Center.)

Traders were not the only people who used the Santa Fe Trail. For example, in September 1846, the Mormon Battalion followed the Cimarron Route near this location in Cimarron County north of Boise City to take and control what became the American Southwest. With Col. Stephen W. Kearney, they left Iowa in July 1846 and walked 2,000 miles to San Diego—the longest march by US infantry at that time.

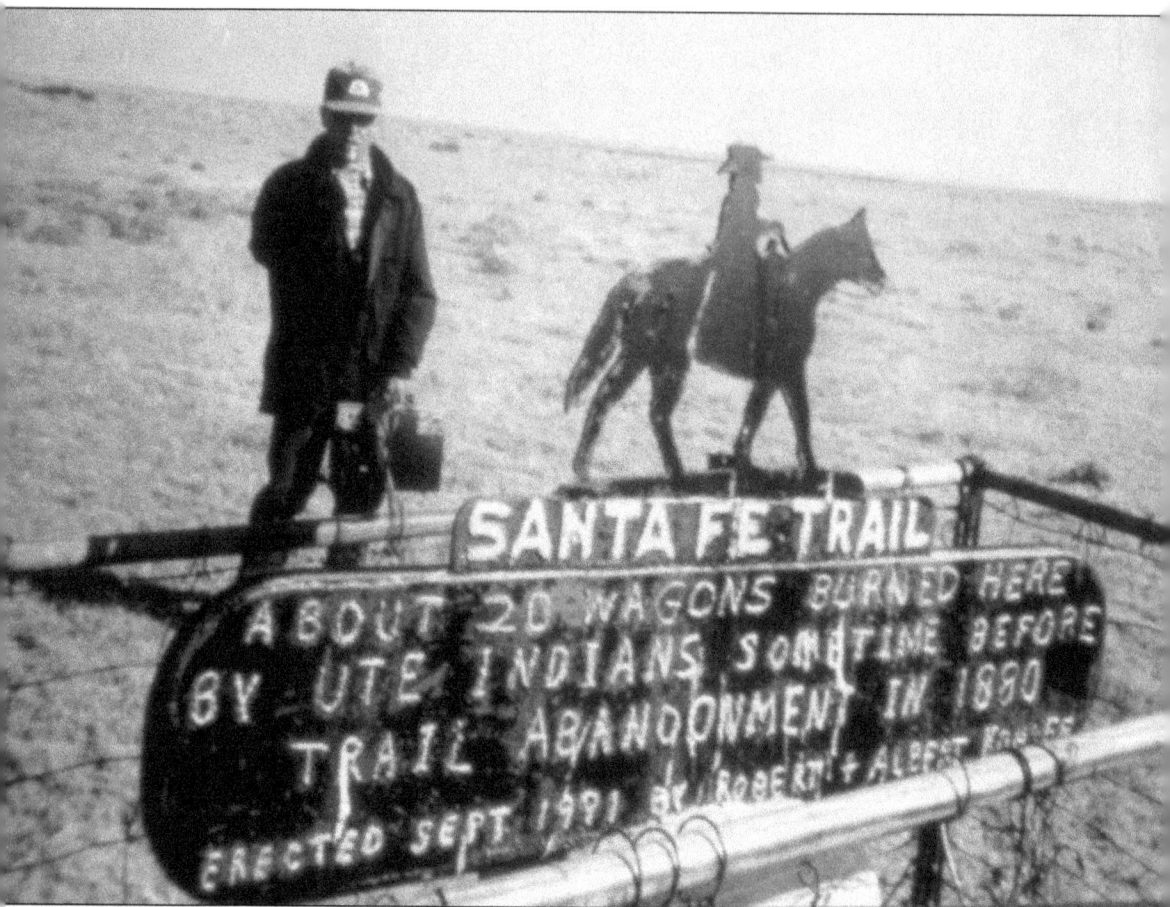

The Santa Fe Trail was strictly a western economic route, not a settlement route for pioneers. On a tour of the Cimarron Route—also called the Cimarron Cut-Off—of the Santa Fe Trail, Morris Alexander tells the history of the trail in Cimarron County at Trujillo Springs, east of Wolf Mountain. Here, in 1880, the official final year of the Santa Fe Trail, Comanche and Ute Indians attacked a wagon train bound for New Mexico. During World War II, local citizens gathered the remnants of the destroyed and forgotten wagons and contributed the metal to the war effort. Located north and east of Boise City, Trujillo Springs is named for a sheep camp established by Mexican herders who lived in the area. There are still rock walls of a corral and buildings at the remote location.

Flag Spring, also known as Upper Spring, is approximately 15 miles north of Boise City. This watering hole along the Santa Fe Trail proved one of the few reliable water sources on the Cimarron Route. Because the spot was in a depression, it was difficult to locate in the undulating terrain. Therefore, traders and travelers erected a tall pole with a flag at the top. Because the Panhandle wind blows constantly, they could easily spy the flying flag. One woman, Ernestine Huning, who traveled the trail with her husband on their way to Santa Fe, recorded in her diary that this particular place along the trail was beautiful because of the lush grass and lovely colorful prairie wildflowers. (Courtesy Cimarron Heritage Center.)

This remote, lush, and rather well-shaded meadow on private property west of Autograph Rock in Cimarron County served as a location where people too ill to continue traveling along the Santa Fe Trail's Cimarron Route were left to die. Many travelers on all western trails would become ill and die quickly of cholera or other highly contagious diseases. Usually, a "watcher" stayed until the ill-fated traveler died; the watcher then buried the body and hurried to catch up with the wagon train that left them in the first place. The watcher was always in danger of encountering Indians. Medicine and healing skills did not exist along western trails of the 19th century, so thousands of pioneers and traders are buried in unmarked graves alongside the trails that they had hoped would take them to great riches, new homes, or personal fulfillment.

Etched names and images decorate this sandstone rock cliff called Autograph Rock in Cimarron County. Signature Rock and Autograph Rock along the Cimarron Route of the Santa Fe Trail bear mute witness of travelers, traders, and soldiers who followed the trail between 1821 and 1880 taking goods to and from Santa Fe and who opened the American Southwest to settlement. The earliest inscription is from 1826, when T. Potts engraved his name. The name that appears the most is F.B. Delgado. At these locations, traders found reliable water, shade trees, and good grazing. American traders used the trail to go west, but Mexican traders pushed mules and took silver and furs east to trade. Many young Mexican ladies traveled the Santa Fe Trail in order to attend finishing schools in the East.

These rocks are all that are left of Fort Nichols in Cimarron County. Midway between Fort Dodge and Santa Fe, Nichols lasted only the summer of 1865. Col. Christopher "Kit" Carson thought he had established the post in New Mexico, for there is little to distinguish the Panhandle from New Mexico. As settlers moved in, they removed rocks and timbers from Fort Nichols to make their own homes. (Courtesy of Johnnie Davis.)

Along the Oklahoma and New Mexico line, Robert McNees and Daniel Monroe scouted for a wagon train bound for Missouri on the Cimarron Route in 1828. Finding good grazing, they took a nap, but Comanche Indians attacked. McNees died at the scene, while Monroe lived for a few days after being rescued. Since then, this location near Corrumpa Creek has been known as McNees' Crossing.

Cimarron County's Carrizo Creek sometimes runs over the road at the entrance of Black Mesa State Park. However, the creek is often dry. The water makes a lovely impression and quite a splash when driven through. Carrizo provides the water for Lake Carl G. Etling, the county's only "lake." A destination for campers, the park provides wonderful sightseeing, good hiking, nice fishing, and rock climbing.

At Black Mesa, geologists say that the short grass prairie meets the Rocky Mountains and therefore call the region the "geologic wonder of the North American continent." From Oklahoma's highest point on Black Mesa, New Mexico rests a mere 443 yards away, Colorado just 4.7 miles away, Texas 31 miles away, and Kansas a distant 53 miles away. Travel on scenic dirt roads is strongly discouraged in the winter or when storms threaten. (Courtesy Levi McGee.)

As a team, these men check out the terrain for the perfect place to situate the future location of Lake Carl G. Etling in Black Mesa State Park. The Oklahoma Department of Tourism and Recreation completed the project in 1959 and named the lake for an Oklahoma state representative. In the early years of the 21st century, the lake was drained for repairs and renovations. A campground, picnic tables, and cabins provide tourists a great place to enjoy Mother Nature in the Panhandle. The lake has a 200-acre surface and offers fishermen good trout fishing except from November through February when the lake is closed to fishing. (Above, Courtesy Cimarron Heritage Center.)

Sparsely covered mesas dot Black Mesa country. Some five million years ago, a Colorado volcano, now extinct and named Piney Point, spewed enough lava to create Black Mesa. The mesa is nearly 30 miles long and extends from Colorado and into Oklahoma; some of it lies in New Mexico. (Courtesy Levi McGee.)

These animals find good grazing and water in the shadow of Black Mesa. The country supports ranching, for the rocky terrain and little water do not support farming. In the late 20th century, a few locals attempted growing vineyards but found little success. For people who want to get away from it all, Black Mesa is the perfect destination. (Courtesy Levi McGee.)

Use a little imagination to see the profile of a stone-faced spinster on the left side of the rock. Old Maid Rock rests north of State Highway 325 leading into Kenton and is one of many unique geologic features in the Black Mesa region. A trip to Cimarron County is not complete without witnessing this Oklahoma Panhandle icon. (Courtesy Tito Aznar.)

Nature also carved the Wedding Party, or Three Sisters, east of Black Mesa and Kenton. Again, one's imagination can make out a towering rock minister on the right standing before a rock bride, groom, and wedding group. This shot from more than 20 years ago shows the wind-eroded rock well; today, the formation is hidden by scrub cedars that have grown around the rock group. (Courtesy Cimarron Heritage Museum.)

At Black Mesa, visitors find many unique geographic features such as Steamboat Mountain, also known as Battleship Mountain. This photograph was taken from the first cabin plane to fly over Cimarron County in 1928. (Courtesy Cimarron Heritage Center.)

More of Mother Nature's handiwork can be seen in this natural rock arch in the Black Mesa region. The opening is certainly wide enough to allow horse-drawn wagons to pass through it. Other rock formations in the area include Castle Rock and Wedding Cake—and yes, couples have tied the knot atop Wedding Cake. (Courtesy Cimarron Heritage Center.)

Tom Lewis climbs the rugged, eight-mile trail up Black Mesa. At the top, an old ammunition box holds the Black Mesa ledger that successful hikers sign to prove they made it. Because the top is quite flat, it is difficult to find the trail again to climb down, so a tall wooden post marks the spot so hikers will not get lost. (Courtesy Charla Lewis.)

Atop Black Mesa, this 11-foot granite obelisk indicates the highest point of elevation in Oklahoma: 4,972.97 feet. The mesa is part of the 549-acre Black Mesa State Park. The Jenkin Lloyd Jones family of Tulsa provided funding for the marker, designed by J.R. Willis and crafted by the Granite Monument Works of Granite, Oklahoma. It was erected by state highway workers in 1928. (Courtesy Cimarron Heritage Center.)

For years, the Panhandle had no law, and outlaws reigned. Near Black Mesa, "Captain" William "Bill" Coe and his gang of 30 to 50 men built Robbers' Roost and Robbers' Fort. The fort had rifle portholes, a fireplace, a piano, and cannon. A nearby cave, Robbers' Roost, hid their loot and horses. A female friend turned Coe in, and vigilantes hung him in Pueblo, Colorado, in 1868. (Courtesy Charla Lewis.)

Here are the remains of Robbers' Fort. To make their living, outlaws rustled cattle and sheep and attacked Santa Fe–bound wagons. They tended to their horses' needs in a canyon still called Blacksmith's Canyon. Students in Dr. Harold Kachel's Panhandle archeology class are seen inspecting the site in the summer of 2009. Wearing white trousers, Kachel stands on the left side of the photograph. (Courtesy Harold Kachel.)

Kevin, Debbie, and Pauline Richter stand at the easy-to-find tri-state marker that represents the point where New Mexico, Colorado, and Oklahoma meet in northwestern Cimarron County. The county is unique in that it is the only one in the United States that abuts four states: Kansas, Texas, New Mexico, and Colorado.

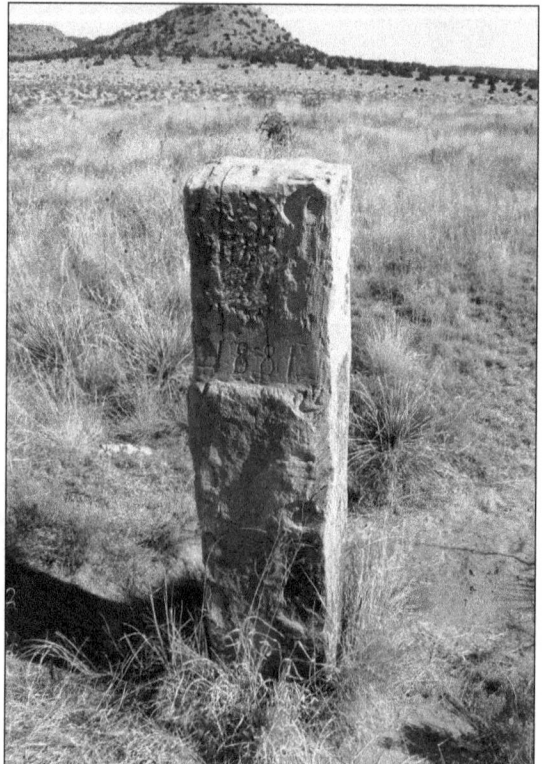

Here stands the original tri-state rock marker that indicates exactly where the borders of Oklahoma, New Mexico, and Colorado touch. The survey marking the spot—37ºN, 103ºW—occurred in 1881, and the marker was set in 1886. This marker rests about 300 yards northeast of the tri-state marker.

People call these animals antelope, but there are no antelope in North America; these animals are pronghorns, and their numbers are increasing in the Panhandle, a fact that distresses farmers. Pronghorns damage fences as they go under and not over them. The only place to hunt pronghorn in Oklahoma is in Cimarron County and far western Texas County. (Courtesy Larry Wiggins.)

The Black Mesa region supports much wildlife, including cougars, bobcats, prairie dogs, elk, badgers, foxes, black bears, mule ear deer, bighorn sheep, whitetail deer, golden eagles, and 200 other species of birds. Black Mesa State Park protects 23 rare species of plants, eight rare species of animals, and four communities of grasses. (Courtesy Cimarron Heritage Center.)

The Okie-Tex Star Party occurs each October near Black Mesa. Hundreds of stargazers bring their camping gear and travel trailers and set up their sophisticated telescopes to do some sky watching. The far northwest reaches of Cimarron County provide one of the darkest places on the earth to investigate the night skies. Volunteer cooks from Boise City provide wonderful meals for the dedicated astronomers. (Courtesy Tito Aznar.)

Just east of Kenton, this remote stage becomes part of the yearly Easter pageant. The event began in 1952 when churches in Colorado, New Mexico, and Oklahoma staged the Passion of Christ amid rocks and hills that look remarkably like the Holy Land. Speakers, singers, and instrumentalists sit below this stage while actors mime the action. Spectators stand on the steep hillside below. (Courtesy Tito Aznar.)

This cliff face contains copper. In the early 1900s, prospectors came to extract copper and coal but had given up by 1910. There were not enough natural resources to make mining prosperous, and the area was too remote. Legend has it that a diamond mine exists somewhere out there. The riches of the Panhandle lay not in silver and gold but in the beauty of its landscape and people.

This is the last building of Mineral City, which was several miles northeast of Fort Nichols. In 1885, men from Kingman, Kansas, built a two-story rock building to attract others to develop coal mining. They carted construction lumber more than 120 miles from southeast Colorado. By 1888, Mineral City had a post office, a general store, and a hotel, but by 1911, the community had vanished. (Courtesy Harold Kachel.)

This historical marker on a corner east of the courthouse in Boise City memorializes the only US soil bombed during World War II—by American pilots. Early on July 5, 1943, misguided B-17 bombers from the Dalhart Army Air Base in Texas dropped a payload of 100-pound practice bombs filled with sand mixed with gunpowder onto the courthouse lawn. No one was hurt, but the incident jarred a lot of people out of bed.

It is difficult to believe that the treeless far western reaches of Cimarron County are actually part of a national forest. These grasslands, a little southwest of Felt, are part of the Rita Blanca Grasslands, one of 20 US grasslands. Rita Blanca is under the direction of the Cibola National Forest; therefore, legally, there is a forest in the 'handle. (Courtesy Tito Aznar.)

As this photograph indicates, not much remains of the federally funded Keyes helium extracting plant. The world's largest at the time, it cost $12 million to build and opened in Cimarron County in 1959 to process 290 million cubic feet annually. In the mid-1900s, the Panhandle's helium resources were the best in the free world at a rich two percent. (Courtesy Tito Aznar.)

Texas County, the middle of the three Panhandle counties, is known as the saddle bronc capital of the world thanks to Robert and Billy Etbauer. The brothers have quite a reputation in the sport of rodeo, with six National Finals Rodeo titles between the two of them in the 1990s.

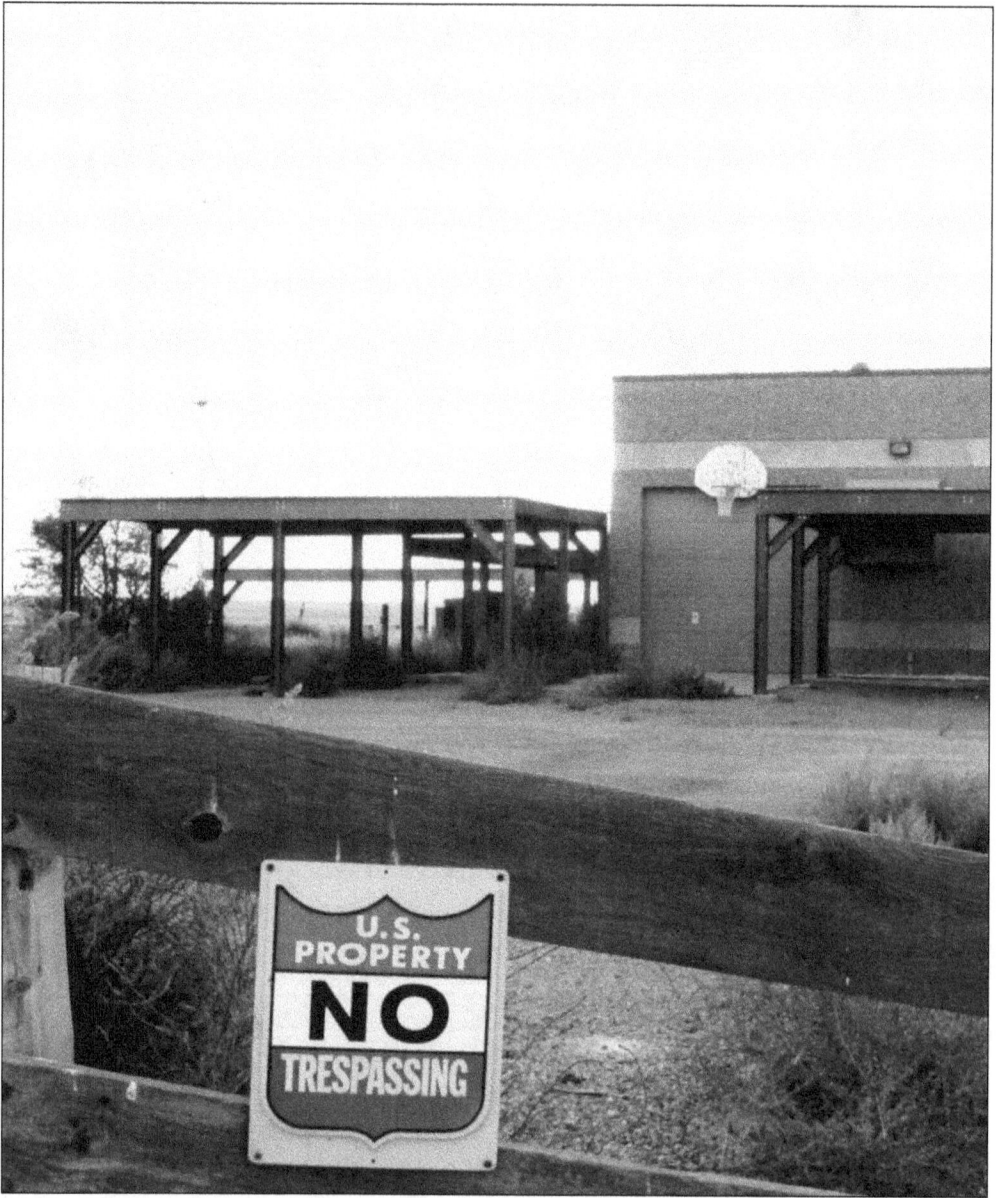

From November 1990 until February 2010, a LORAN (Long Range Navigation) Coast Guard station was in full service southwest of Felt in Cimarron County. In February 2010, the Coast Guard terminated all LORAN stations because of the 2010 Department of Homeland Security Appropriations Act supporting Pres. Barack Obama's desire that the federal government shed unneeded federal programs. Originally, LORAN provided radio-navigation aid for US coastal waters and then included the continental United States as well. Twenty-four such stations across the nation offered navigation, location, and timing aids for civil and military air, land, and marine uses. The Boise City LORAN station, as this installation was called, received a commendation in 1991 for its operational service, diligent work, and help in establishing other LORAN locations. There seems to be few places more landlocked and water deprived than the 'handle, so the presence of the Coast Guard assumes the profile of legend and myth—or at the very least, irony. (Courtesy Tito Aznar.)

Cactus is a typical plant in the dry climate of the Panhandle. A cactus commonly called the cholla is really the buckhorn cholla (*Opuntia acanthocarpa*). It grows well in the sandy soil of the High Plains. Legend has it that the cholla "throws" its spines at its victims, but that just is not so. The narrow-leaved, tall, and thin yucca (*Yucca angustissima*), with its white, spiky summer blooms, decorates roadsides, pastures, and neighborhoods. Other plants common to the Panhandle include the prickly pear cactus (*Nopal opuntia*) and the Oklahoma state wildflower, gaillardia or Indian blanket (*Gaillardia pulchella*). These and other wildflowers make the Panhandle very colorful in the spring and summer. (Both courtesy of Harold Kachel.)

The little town of Texhoma sits astride Texas and Oklahoma—the only community to have that distinction. Texhoma has often used its "dual citizenship" as a promotional tool. A centerpiece of the town is its three-flag display on its main thoroughfare, Second Street, where the flags of the United States, Texas, and Oklahoma fly. Those unfamiliar with Oklahoma in general, and the Panhandle in particular, assume that Lake Texhoma, a large and popular recreational lake in south central Oklahoma, is near the town of Texhoma in Texas County, but this is not the case. (Above, courtesy Texhoma Historical Society and Museum.)

Beaver, the county seat of Beaver County, hosts the World Champion Cow Chip Throwing Competition every summer. Needless to say, there is no other such competition in the world, and there are always plenty of chips to throw in such wide-open spaces populated by lots of cattle. Originally called Beaver City, the town takes its name from the Beaver River that flows on the north side of town.

Cattle feed yards like this one, Tri-State Feeders south of Turpin in Beaver County, fatten cattle for packinghouses. Cattle are kept until they reach optimum weight in order to fetch the highest price for their owners, who then sell them to packers. A full one-sixth of the beef cattle in the country live on rangeland or in cattle-feeding operations such as this one on the Great Plains.

Standing in the bottom of what is supposed to be Lake Optima, hikers can see the lake's dam. Unfortunately, what started out as a good idea turned bad when the Army Corps of Engineers situated the lake over porous bedrock in the 1960s. The agricultural use of the underground water supply, the Ogallala Aquifer, has impacted the amount of water in the lake as well. Therefore, the lake has never even approached being full, as any water that does collect seeps away. The location hosts a wide variety of flora and fauna however. The earthen dam is one of the longest in the world, but unfortunately it is no longer open to visitors or sightseers. The boat ramp below does not come anywhere near water. Recently, with much controversy, Lake Optima was closed permanently. (Both courtesy Charla Lewis.)

The Race Across America was once known as America's toughest bicycle race, and it traced through the Panhandle on Highway 270/3/412. The last race occurred in 1996, with the winner receiving a top prize of $75,000. The 2,905-mile race began in Irvine, California, and ended in Savannah, Georgia, with Slapout in eastern Beaver County as the halfway point. Support vehicles and personnel accompanied each of the competitors to help with bike repairs and to provide the racers with food, water, and medical attention. There are not many turns on the highway, but the long and low hills of the Panhandle would sometimes make the bicyclists struggle. The heat of the summer sun and the constant Panhandle wind can also make pedaling difficult and tiring. Even a settlement as small as Slapout would be a welcome sight and a relief to the competitors. (Courtesy Michael Ask.)

Most people think that the Oklahoma Panhandle is simply flat, flatter, and flattest, but they are wrong. People are always surprised to see sights like this, for the Panhandle boasts various forms of terrain, including canyons, mesas, plains, and sand dunes. These sand dunes are some of many at Beaver Dunes State Park in Beaver County. Formed by the constant Panhandle winds and the ever-changing Beaver River over millions of years, the sand dunes attract outdoors lovers, four-wheeler aficionados, dirt bike riders, and campers who enjoy the park's 520 acres. The state park began as the Beaver City Park, established in 1930.

There are many people who do not believe that beautiful water spots exist in the Oklahoma Panhandle; they do, but there are not many of them. This photograph proves that there is at least one pretty water location—the Beaver River in Beaver Dunes State Park. At the park, visitors can actually see water in the river, which is something that cannot be said for other places along the river. The Beaver River State Park, with its Sahara-like sand dunes, coupled with the river is certainly a study in Oklahoma contrasts.

If one does not like the weather in the 'handle, wait, and it will change soon. Once in a while, after a thunderstorm, dust blows. On occasion, people will wear shorts shortly after a blizzard. Thankfully, tornadoes do not appear very frequently, but they sometimes ravage the countryside, especially during the spring and early summer. This tornado swept through Texas County on June 7, 1941. (Courtesy Texhoma Historical Society and Museum.)

The Panhandle never seems to have enough water, and the area is famous for its dust storms. People find water where it is not supposed to be but are hard-pressed to find water where it is supposed to be. The Panhandle's only lake, Carl G. Etling, does not contain much water, but this "lake" is actually the Oklahoma Panhandle State University Golf Course after a rare thunderstorm. (Courtesy Charla Lewis.)

The Panhandle's water problem is seen here. Sometimes the Panhandle gets too much of a good thing as this 1915 Texhoma flood illustrates. Average yearly rainfall averages less than 18 inches. The lowest recorded rainfall fell in 1956, when Cimarron County received 6.5 inches. On average, the Panhandle sees rain less than 50 days each year. (Courtesy Texhoma Historical Society and Museum.)

From this bridge west of Boise City, travelers can see the riverbed of the Beaver River, here covered with a light dusting of snow. Development of irrigation, farm and community wells, and farm ponds has stopped the flow of the river that never ran very deep. One woman traveling the Cimarron Route of the Santa Fe Trail in the mid-19th century commented that she was not worried about crossing the Beaver, as no one had ever drowned in it.

Winters are usually mild, but it can snow—a lot. The photograph above shows Texhoma blanketed with snow in the winter of 1911–1912. In Beaver that winter, 87 inches of snow fell. Other bad winters came in 1918–1919, 1943–1944, and 1957. When drifts dramatically pile up, as they do because of the strong Panhandle winds, helicopters drop hay to far-flung cattle herds and medicine to residents in remote locations. The most recent blizzard occurred in December 2009 and greatly affected western Cimarron County. Frank Dinkler, a "downstater" from Oklahoma City, was shocked by the snow that he saw in Goodwell. The good thing about snowstorms in the Panhandle is the short time that it takes the snow to melt. Icing proves far more treacherous than snow does. (Above, courtesy Texhoma Historical Society and Museum.)

Grass grows thicker in a light-colored depression—evidence of the Jones-Plummer Trail south of Beaver. Traders Ed Jones and Joe Plummer blazed this trail in 1874 from their trading post on Wolf Creek in the Texas Panhandle to Dodge City. Not much of the trail remains; this rare extant portion is on the property of Harold and Joan Kachel.

This photograph from the late 1800s captures a freighter, his wagon, and horse team travelling the Jones-Plummer Trail. Supplies, buffalo hides, and buffalo bones provided most of the freight during the life of the trail. Soldiers followed the trail, especially during the 1870s when the Plains Indians were defeated and placed on reservations. (Courtesy Jones-Plummer Trail Museum.)

These images come from pages of the official Cimarron Territory ledger book, wherein delegates to the convention to create this new US territory wrote their constitution and laws and signed their names. Cimarron Territory never became a reality, even though Beaver residents fought hard for the special designation. This is the only known stamp of the seal for the proposed territory. The seal itself got lost when Fred Tracy, one of the leaders of the failed movement, left it by mistake on a train in Kingfisher, Oklahoma, in the 1880s on the way to donate it to a museum in Guthrie, Oklahoma. The ledger rests in the No Man's Land Museum in Goodwell. (Both courtesy Tito Aznar.)

Members of a construction crew handle teams and wagons and equipment to build a road near Forgan in Beaver County in 1914. Early roads were of course dirt, perhaps with some gravel, and often had highfalutin names, such as the Great Plains Road, the Atlantic Pacific Highway, and the Dallas, Canadian, Denver Highway. (Courtesy Jones-Plummer Museum.)

Men pave the first road in Cimarron County in 1933. Initially, roads were primitive mail routes, some 60 miles long. Increased recreation and tourism demanded additional paved roads. Today, Highways 412, 283, 64, 54, and 3 wind through the Panhandle. Highway 3, called the Heritage Trail by infamous Oklahoma governor Bill Murray, has three names: Northwest Passage, 45th Infantry Division Highway, and Governor George Nigh Highway. (Courtesy Cimarron Heritage Center.)

US Highway 54 carries many "snowbirds," retirees who travel from permanent homes in northern states to warmer climates, such as Arizona or Southern California, for the winter. Many pull their homes away from home with them, just like pioneers and traders who traversed the region before them. During the late fall and early spring, their dollars spent on lodging and fuel contribute to the Panhandle economy.

Many semi-trucks pass through the Panhandle. A major national thoroughfare, US Highway 54, goes through the Panhandle as it stretches between Mexico and Canada. Because all Panhandle highways have few grades or sharp turns and no bridges or underpasses for trucks and their drivers to negotiate, the Panhandle sees a lot of big-rig loads—long, wide, heavy, and tall—with their escort vehicles leading the way.

The Panhandle suffered terribly during the 1930s, when ill-fated farming practices, drought, overproduction, and high winds blew in dust storms. Mountainous dust clouds affected physical and mental health, incomes, agriculture, and population. The Panhandle saw the worst of the storms and suffered the greatest population decline. The dust caused a new disease to develop; dust pneumonia took the lives of the young and the elderly. (Courtesy Cimarron Heritage Center.)

The worst duster hit on Palm Sunday, April 14, 1935, known as Black Sunday, and many believed it to be the end of the world. This is the way it looked in Cimarron County that day. Some storms lasted six hours, and thick dust extinguished lamps and stoves due to a lack of oxygen. (Courtesy Cimarron Heritage Museum.)

This shot captures the aftermath of a 1930s dust storm in Cimarron County. During a duster, dust became so thick that people could not see their hands in front of their faces. Some folks caught in dust storms temporarily lost their vision. After one storm, a family noted bumps in the road outside their farmhouse. They discovered that the bumps were chickens blown from the henhouse, suffocated by the dust, and then buried in the blowing dust. (Courtesy Cimarron Heritage Museum.)

This 1930s duster hit Hooker in Texas County. During the Dust Bowl, women had difficulty finding a clear day to wash. Some people scooped dirt out of their homes with shovels. The weight of dust on picture frames caused them to fall off walls. In Goodwell, at Panhandle A&M College, collected dust caused a stairwell to collapse in Anna Jarvis Hall, the women's dormitory, in 1938. (Courtesy ArVel White.)

These dust clouds billow in Beaver County in 1935. Strong grain prices in the 1920s encouraged farmers to convert more prairie to grow wheat, thereby destroying the topsoil. With the soil uncovered, strong winds blew it away. Bad farming practices and climate change created the Dust Bowl. The little annual rainfall decreased during the 1930s, so that pasture and crops would not grow. (Courtesy Jones-Plummer Museum.)

Growing a successful garden during the Dust Bowl years was not easy. This woman babies vegetables in her Texas County garden. Folks depended on garden "truck" for their own tables and sold excess as a way of making a few extra dimes or traded garden items for commodities in town. (Courtesy Cimarron Heritage Center.)

The 1950s saw dust storms as well. This Cimarron County photograph was taken on April 22, 1956, by Ralph S. Murphy, and illustrates wind erosion where soil conservation was not practiced. The National Resources Conservation Service investigated farming practices and wind erosion. Photographs such as this documented another drought disaster. During the 21st century, the Panhandle has lacked rainfall, but there is currently no evidence of another Dust Bowl. However, people say another will arrive if significant rains do not fall. (Courtesy Cimarron Heritage Center.)

The Ogallala Aquifer has been the lifesaving blood for the Oklahoma Panhandle and much of the Great Plains as well. This underground water supply provides water for the irrigation of crops via these center pivot irrigation systems. Experts say that there is just 50 years' worth of water left in the aquifer, and after that, the Panhandle will be worthless for agriculture.

Two

PEOPLE OF
THE PANHANDLE

People who have stayed to make their livings in the Panhandle know how difficult it really is. Historically, the Oklahoma Panhandle has had little to offer—not even law and order in the 19th century—so it was not a very safe place to bring a family. The Panhandle is short on water and rain, even in good years. Pioneers realized these things, and when they added to these concerns the presence of fierce, nomadic Indians, they realized that the Panhandle was not a very attractive place to settle.

Even today, some lament the lack of mall shopping, cultural entertainment, lovely and lush landscapes, cities, exciting activities, water sports, and fine dining as drawbacks to living in the Panhandle. However, people have made the Panhandle the agricultural and economic center that it is today. Residents revel in being from a part of the country that nobody wanted and know that they must be stalwart, resolute, and resourceful in order to stay here. The Panhandle is not everyone's cup of tea, but those who call it home defend and appreciate it and are good stewards of the land. The pioneer spirit is alive among those who live in the Oklahoma Panhandle.

In the 1870s, James Lane built a trading post at the halfway point of the Jones-Plummer Trail in what became Beaver. Here, traders and cowboys on the way to Wolf Creek in Texas or to Dodge City could spend the night under a real roof, eat food not prepared over a campfire, and purchase supplies. Of course, the aluminum windows are not original.

A typical freighter poses with his team and wagon near the Beaver City Bank. Beaver City, because of politically savvy businessmen, became the leading Panhandle community before statehood. In 1887, it fomented the movement to turn the Panhandle into Cimarron Territory. This plan failed, and the Panhandle was unilaterally attached to Oklahoma when Oklahoma became the 46th state on November 16, 1907. (Courtesy Jones-Plummer Museum.)

This Beaver County sod house is typical of the Great Plains and the High Plains. Pioneers found few trees but plenty of grass; therefore, they carved sod to use instead of timber to build homes and barns. This particular homestead sat between Forgan and Beaver in 1886. (Courtesy Jones-Plummer Museum.)

Jacob Cook, his family, and some of their horses pose outside their Beaver County home near Elmwood around 1900. The Cooks' home features elements of both types of dwellings typical on the prairie, as it is a dugout with a sod roof. Elmwood sits on a rise and is about 20 miles south of Beaver. Today, it has a single business—a convenience store. (Courtesy Jones-Plummer Museum.)

The family of Ben Hayden poses outside their sod home in Beaver County near Blue Mound School in 1906. Note the big hole on the left side of the photograph where the sod has been removed to build the house. The Hayden family received their mail at Anthony, another little community that no longer exists. (Courtesy Jones-Plummer Museum.)

In 1906, J.A. Alexander proved up a Cimarron County homestead. Alexander's dugout was unique, with a covered entryway and a wooden roof. If a dugout's roof were not well marked, a cow, horse, buffalo, or human leg might come through it, so settlers stuck flags on their roofs, fenced them, or planted flowers on them so that they would stand out from the rest of the prairie. (Courtesy Cimarron Heritage Center.)

After securing homesteads, settlers "proved them up" with a barn, a home, and tilled ground. Here, Etta Wilson plows virgin sod in Texas County in the early 1900s. Developed in the mid-1800s, this single one-way plow turned the soil in one direction and did not allow for the mixing of soil, seed, moisture, and fertilizer. This plowing method contributed to the Dust Bowl. (Courtesy Texhoma Historical Society and Museum.)

This coal bucket contains dried cow manure. With few trees, everyone who traveled through or homesteaded until the early 20th century relied on what buffalo, cattle, mules, and horses had left behind. Cow chips burn quickly with a lot of heat, making them perfect for campfires. People did not like gathering chips, not so much because they objected to picking up dung, but because of the creepy crawlies beneath them.

This photograph captures a double date in Texas County in the early 1900s and illustrates how people courted before the days of the horseless carriage. Long rides in the countryside could be romantic. As a new bride in May 1908, Caroline Henderson recalled the trip from Guymon back to her cabin in Cimarron County as a "perfect night of moonlight and starlight." (Courtesy Texhoma Historical Society and Museum.)

Residents have always been very good at making the Oklahoma Panhandle bloom and have succeeded in growing a wealth of successful crops through the years. In this 1909 photograph, volunteers, including children, pose on Jim Crabtree's farm. They had just harvested broomcorn to make money to build a new Christian church in Beaver County. They made $600 for their harvesting efforts. Benjamin Franklin first introduced broomcorn to the American colonies. Beginning in the early 1900s, it became for years the sole ingredient for brooms worldwide, mainly because of the amount of broomcorn grown in the Panhandle. There were many broom makers in the Panhandle during that time, and those companies employed many women. Broomcorn sold for $200 per ton in 1905 and was a staple agricultural product at the time. (Courtesy Jones-Plummer Museum.)

These workers harvest a bountiful 1915 hay crop outside of Forgan in Beaver County. Hay was and is an important agricultural commodity in the Oklahoma Panhandle, for farmers can use the hay for their own cattle and horse herds and sell hay to others for the same purposes. Thank goodness technology has improved through the years. (Courtesy Jones-Plummer Museum.)

On a Texhoma street, one man proudly shows off his garden's bounty of sweet potatoes in Texas County in 1911. Gardening has always been a part of the rural life, providing food for the gardeners' tables and some extra income as well if sold at typical farmers' markets. (Courtesy Texhoma Historical Society and Museum.)

Wheat harvest on Guy Hume's farm in Cimarron County in the early 1900s needed many hands and draft animals and primitive equipment compared to the high-tech equipment used by farmers today. Always an excellent agricultural producer, the Panhandle ranks nationally in farm and ranch production. For example, Texas County consistently ranks in the top five counties in the nation in wheat and cattle production. (Courtesy Cimarron Heritage Center.)

Wheat is a mainstay of Panhandle farming, as it grows well even as a dryland crop. Before mechanized wheat harvesting became a reality, farmers would line up their teams and grain wagons at the B.O. Cator Grain Company in Texhoma to sell their grain. From the elevator, wheat could be easily loaded into railroad grain cars and sent anywhere. (Courtesy Texhoma Historical Society and Museum.)

When the railroad came to Texhoma in 1901, even Texas wheat growers took advantage of it. Texas farmers in nearby counties like Hansford took their grain to Texhoma, for the elevator there was closer than many in Texas. In the photograph above, Texas farmers using a Peerless U1 tractor (a tractor with a double-geared steam engine) efficiently freight their crop to Texhoma in 1911 by pulling many grain wagons at once. Below, the summer wheat harvest of 1942 is pictured. Some 75 farmers line up their wheat trucks to be weighed and to get paid before depositing their crop in the Texhoma grain elevator. (Both courtesy Texhoma Historical Society and Museum.)

These bales of cotton came from the first fields of cotton planted in the Panhandle in Texas County in late 1924; however, the Dust Bowl of the 1930s squashed the production of cotton. History does repeat itself, for almost a century later, some Panhandle farmers have once again decided to plant cotton. The photograph below shows bales from a Cimarron County cotton field in late 2010. Gins pick up the bales, but such attention increases production costs. The nearest cotton gin is in the Texas Panhandle, north of Dumas. (Above, courtesy Texhoma Historical Society and Museum; below, Debbie Richter.)

The photograph above shows a rather primitive-looking early oil-drilling rig in Beaver County and proves just how far technology in the oil and gas exploration business has come in a mere century. The photograph at left is of a wooden derrick that rises over the first oil well near Texhoma in Texas County in August 1919; it was dubbed Allison No. 1. Oil exploration and its support services continue to play a vital role in the economy of the Panhandle. (Above, courtesy Jones-Plummer Museum; at left, Texhoma Historical Society and Museum.)

Today, modern and efficient oil-drilling rigs dot the landscape as drilling companies still seek to tap the Panhandle's underground natural resources. The Hugoton Gas Field under southwest Kansas and the Panhandle is the largest natural gas field in the country and the fifth largest in the world. It was discovered and first tapped in the late 1950s.

Warren Petroleum, a pioneer in liquefied petroleum gas (LPG), a byproduct of crude oil, built 20 plants in the United States, including the Mocane plant in Beaver County. It opened in 1950, employed 22 workers, and processed 210 million cubic feet of gas daily by 1961. Butane and propane were not commodities before the 1920s, but Warren perfected extracting, processing, transporting, and storing it in the 1950s. (Courtesy Jones-Plummer Museum.)

An example of the many politically active residents of Beaver City, Fred Tracy took a lead role in the attempt to make the Oklahoma Panhandle its own US territory—Cimarron Territory. In addition, Tracy represented the Panhandle at the Oklahoma State Constitutional Convention (1906–1907) in Oklahoma City. (Courtesy Jones-Plummer Museum.)

After serving as the associate editor for newspaper editor Noah Daves for two years, a young Maude O. Thomas became the owner and publisher of the Beaver newspaper, the *Old Beaver Herald*, in February 1902. Here, she is hard at work producing an issue of the weekly newspaper. Beaver became a town in 1883, and prior to statehood, it was quite the hotbed of politics and business for No Man's Land. (Courtesy Jones-Plummer Museum.)

This photograph was taken on August 25, 1899, and features Dudley C. Sloan, who is sitting astride the white-faced horse facing the camera on the left side. He worked as a cowboy on the T.O. James Ranch on Coldwater Creek in Sherman County, Texas. This image captures Dudley on the morning of his 21st birthday. To celebrate, on August 24, he rode 60 miles from the James Ranch to near a little community called Optima in Texas County to attend a dance. The people in this photograph had all danced the night away and posed the next morning before they went home. Sloan eventually owned ranches in Beaver County and near Kenton in far western Cimarron County and even became a county sheriff there. (Courtesy No Man's Land Museum.)

Neva Powell Sloan and her daughter Berniece stand in the open doorway of their home on the Dudley Sloan Ranch in Beaver County in 1906. The Cimarron River flood of 1914 destroyed the home, and this photograph is one of a few possessions that survived the disaster. (Courtesy No Man's Land Museum.)

This May 1, 1914, photograph includes three Sloan children—Mary, William, and Raymond—the morning after the Cimarron River swept away their home. With no warning of the flood, the family escaped with only the clothes that they were wearing. The children sit atop one of the many ranch buildings destroyed that fateful night when the usually docile Cimarron turned into a raging river. (Courtesy No Man's Land Museum.)

In the last quarter of the 1800s, cattlemen saw the vast potential of the Panhandle as the perfect place to graze cattle herds. Ranchers shared resources and cowboys in the spring to gather cows and calves, which were then separated into smaller herds belonging to individual ranchers. Cowboys branded calves to prove their ownership. (Courtesy No Man's Land Museum.)

In 1878, Ezra Dudley and son John started the Anchor D on the Beaver River in Texas County. Eventually, their range stretched from Kansas into the Texas Panhandle with 30,000 head of cattle on a million acres. Various families have expanded the brand—T.C. Schumaker, Howard M. Stonebraker, Edwin Zea, R.S. Coon, Lewis Mayer, and Jack Freeman—making it one of the largest ranches in Oklahoma. (Courtesy Tito Aznar.)

This photograph shows part of the vast Hitch Ranch. James K. Hitch ran his herd with the OX brand in the mid-1880s in Texas County. Henry Hitch, his son, took over in 1921, and then Henry Hitch Jr. assumed control in the 1960s. He expanded the operation to include cattle feed yards and hog production, making Hitch Enterprises one of the most influential agricultural businesses in Oklahoma. (Courtesy Chris Hitch.)

This saltbox home served as the Green Ranch headquarters in Texas County. The red sandstone rock used to construct this building and two others on the ranch property was quarried in Texas County. This old home stands not far west of Palo Duro Creek, which runs south into the Texas Panhandle. (Courtesy No Man's Land Museum.)

The wide-open spaces of the Panhandle's High Plains are clear to see in this photograph from the early 1900s. This cattle roundup occurred on the Dimmett Ranch in Texas County. The cattle industry is still a significant player in the Panhandle economy. (Courtesy Texhoma Historical Society and Museum.)

Otto Nicholas Barby and his new bride, May, homesteaded on 160 acres in 1896 in Beaver County to establish what still remains as one of the prominent cattle ranches in the state. The photograph above includes only a portion of the sweeping Barby Ranch. In the image below, swales of an old stage road in Beaver County are visible on the Barby Ranch. Stagecoaches ran between Beaver and Inglewood, Kansas, and crossed the Beaver River at Rock Crossing at the location of the Riverside Post Office. Normally, Riverside did not have a postmaster, so stage drivers simply left mail inside an old stove in the post office building. Eventually, people came by, rifled through the letters and packages to find what belonged to them, and left the rest for others to retrieve.

The cowboys seen above rode for the Palmer Ranch in Cimarron County near Kenton in the early 1900s. Many ranches, such as the 101 Ranch, ran hundreds of head of cattle on their ranges. In the image below, cowboys have roped and "throwed," or flanked, a calf and are about to apply a hot branding iron to its side to mark it as a Palmer beef. The crew's supply wagon is parked on the right. Today, ranching plays an important economic role in the Panhandle and contributes greatly to its economy and the economy of Oklahoma in general. (Both courtesy Bob Phillips and Cimarron Heritage Center.)

In 1902, four working cowboys from a Beaver County ranch pose while playing poker and display their pistols in jest. The quartet sits alongside Kiowa Creek, a tributary of the Beaver River, near a spot known as the Ponds. The gambling group includes, from left to right, Norvel Earl, Charley Ford, Charlie "Shorty" Harris, and Charley Aikens. Charley Ford's brother Bob is credited with shooting outlaw Jesse James in Missouri in 1882. (Courtesy Jones-Plummer Museum.)

During the 1950s and 1960s, Darrell Morris established Sunset Farms in Beaver County on land homesteaded by his forebears in the early 1900s. He featured Angus cattle and wheat fields in his farm and ranch operation. Sunset Farms continues its farming operation in the Panhandle. (Courtesy Troy Morris.)

Sometimes, grain elevators do not have enough storage space for the Panhandle's abundant crops. As a result, it is not unusual to see mountainous piles of wheat, corn, or grain sorghum sitting near grain elevators or alongside railroad tracks; from there, it can be loaded into grain cars and shipped away. Usually, the grain is placed inside fences and may be covered with plastic to protect it from the elements.

A relatively new cash crop in the Panhandle is the sunflower. Its large and cheery yellow and black face follows the track of the sun each day. The seeds of the plant are used to make oil or processed to be enjoyed by nut and seed aficionados, like baseball players. (Courtesy Tito Aznar.)

Not everything that grows in the Panhandle is worth much, like tumbleweeds. They blow about all year—depending which way the wind's blowing. They become a fire hazard when they gather along fencerows, in ditches, or among trees or bushes. Panhandle winds pull dead Russian thistle plants (*Salsola tragus*) from the ground, turning them into tumbleweeds and scattering the seeds of the sticky, brittle weeds.

These young ladies hold rabbits they shot in the early 1920s in Texas County. In the Dust Bowl, rabbits plagued the Panhandle so much that people rounded them up in "rabbit drives" and clubbed them to death to prevent them from eating struggling crops and gardens planted by people desperate to feed themselves during the worst of times. (Courtesy Texhoma Historical Society and Museum.)

Here, some pheasant hunters display their birds after a Texas County winter's morning hunt in the 1950s. Turkey, deer, and pheasant are three favorite hunting seasons that draw hunters into the Panhandle in the fall and winter and boost the region's economy. Typical mild temperatures during these seasons make hunting a very attractive activity. (Courtesy Texhoma Historical Society and Museum.)

Jerry Monzingo (left) and Garrett McCargish kneel beside a deer taken by Jerry in the fall of 2010 in Texas County near Hardesty. Hunters have outstanding opportunities to experience the bounty of the Panhandle, and trophies include deer, pronghorn, pheasant, and turkey. The only place to hunt pronghorn in Oklahoma is in Cimarron County and in western Texas County. There are specialized seasons when hunters may take game with bows and arrows, muzzleloaders, or modern guns. It is easy to spot wildlife in the Panhandle, for coveys of quail, nests of pheasant, herds of deer, or flocks of turkeys (below) can be seen any month of the year. (Above, courtesy Peter Camfield; below, Harold Kachel.)

Three

COMMUNITIES OF THE PANHANDLE

The people of the Panhandle established communities to accommodate their settlement and to foster the settlement of others in the region. The most remote part of Oklahoma, the Panhandle, is surrounded by remote regions of four other states—Colorado, Texas, Kansas, and New Mexico—so settlers and cattlemen in this five-state area traded and traveled back and forth across state and territorial lines. Naturally, towns flourished and died, but others have been tenacious and remained through the tough times at the turn of the century and the Dust Bowl to continue to offer goods, services, and educational centers to citizens.

Population numbers in the Panhandle decreased between 2000 and 2010, as shown by the 16.5 percent decrease in Cimarron County and the 10 percent decrease in Beaver County. Texas County did increase in population by 5.1 percent in that same decade due to the rise in Hispanic immigration numbers. Those declining population numbers hit the Panhandle economy hard and are difficult to recoup. Young people have a tendency to leave rural areas, and this happens in the Panhandle as well. Towns like Keyes and Boise City, Turpin and Hardesty, Beaver and Gate suffer when residents leave for greener pastures. It seems that people in the Panhandle have never really stayed for long, but the towns they built have, for the most part, hung on into the 21st century. What will transpire before the next century comes along is anyone's guess. Oil and gas production, livestock production, and farming enterprises have always been the mainstays of the Panhandle, and towns must exist to support these endeavors. The Panhandle and its communities will survive—probably in a diminished capacity for the most part—but they will endure, serving future generations and our nation in the long run.

The Rock Island Railroad became the lifeline of the Panhandle at the turn of the 20th century. Trackage eventually extended from Liberal, Kansas, to Santa Rosa, New Mexico. As it was laid southwest across the Panhandle, towns grew about 10 miles apart beside it: Tyrone, Hooker, Optima, Guymon, Goodwell, and Texhoma. By 1901, the railroad had made it to the Texas and Oklahoma border and headed out into New Mexico. It was fairly easy to lay the trackage, as there were few rivers or grades to complicate construction. This photograph looks westward down the track toward Texhoma, coming out of Goodwell in Texas County. During the 1920s and 1930s, people traveled between Panhandle towns on the train. Many students who attended Panhandle A&M College at that time commuted daily on the trains that serviced the communities. Today, no passenger trains run in the Panhandle.

Kenton was the unofficial county seat of Cimarron County until an election was conducted in August 1908. Boise City won, so men from Boise City went to Kenton to steal county records. Somebody told Sheriff Dudley Sloan, who sent deputies to protect the documents. A standoff ensued, only ending when someone realized that moving a county seat could not occur until 30 days after the election. (Courtesy Bob Phillips and Cimarron Heritage Center.)

Pictured is the interior of Kenton's Plunkett and Slack General Store. Established in the early 1890s as Florence, Kenton provided services for New Mexico, Colorado, Texas, New Mexico, and Oklahoma. Kenton is the westernmost community in Oklahoma and the only part of Oklahoma that rests inside the Mountain Time Zone. (Courtesy Cimarron Heritage Center.)

Pictured is the interior of the Mercantile, called simply "The Merc." The only business in Kenton, it provides the few locals with basic commodities and contains a panoply of rocks, artifacts, and dinosaur bones found in the area. Even until the 1900s, Kenton catered to local homesteaders with a school, a newspaper, several stores, some churches, a few saloons, and a boardinghouse. It even served as the county seat for a while. Today, there are some homes, two bed-and-breakfast establishments, a museum, a cemetery, and a few churches, but the community's glory days ended over a century ago.

This 1895 photograph shows the interior of a drugstore in Boise City. Two men, Dr. William B. Hall and J.U. Shugart, owned and operated the store housed inside an adobe building on the community's main street. Besides selling patent medicines and creating them, too, it sold toiletries and general merchandise. (Courtesy Cimarron Heritage Center.)

At the Texhoma Speedway in the second decade of the 20th century, racers and mechanics gathered on summer weekends to compete. Fans sat in a grandstand covered with an awning to protect them against the bright and hot Panhandle sun. Nationally, motor racing was very popular at the time. The photograph below captures a moment on July 27, 1916, as drivers prepare for a 150-mile race. The speedway proved to be a popular spot for locals and sat where the Texhoma sale barn sits today on the east side of town. (Both courtesy Texhoma Historical Society and Museum.)

Fans also enjoyed motorcycle racing at the Texhoma racetrack. On July 18, 1916, motorcyclists start a 50-mile race. The early decades of the 20th century were known as the golden age of motorcycling in America, with board tracks being the predominant type of racetrack. The Texhoma Speedway was dirt, not wood, and apparently, Harleys and even side hacks entertained fans. (Courtesy Texhoma Historical Society and Museum.)

The photograph above captures a group of men working to construct buildings on Texhoma's main street, actually Second Street, in the year 1910. Some of these buildings still stand and are occupied today. The photograph below captures the first bank building in Texhoma, which housed the Farmers' State Bank. In addition, it shared its interior space with the National Land Company, which sold parcels of land to those who were eager to establish a farm and home in Texas County. Today, there is a single bank in Texhoma with branches in Guymon and Goodwell. (Both courtesy Texhoma Historical Society and Museum.)

The Thomason family ran a large general mercantile store in Texhoma in the early decades of the 20th century. The Thomason Brothers' general store sold almost anything that Texas County residents could want, as this interior shot of the well-stocked, neat, and commodious store illustrates. Thomason Brothers' Mercantile took up prime real estate on a corner lot on Second Street. Alas, there are no stores of this kind in Texhoma today. (Both courtesy Texhoma Historical Society and Museum.)

A photograph from the early 1900s captures a slice of daily small-town life. A short-order cook in a Texhoma Main Street café serves up a plate of food for a hungry, mid-afternoon customer who peers through the pass-through window. Today, travelers and locals can have a meal at one of three cafés in Texhoma. (Courtesy Texhoma Historical Society and Museum.)

Wearing 18th-century homemade costumes, Texhoma ladies have gathered at the home of Mrs. W. C. Smith for a special event—a George Washington birthday party—in the 1920s. The event and their attire may seem contrived to modern Panhandlers, but entertainment was, and sometimes still is, rather difficult to find. Obviously, Panhandlers can create their own fun. (Courtesy Texhoma Historical Society and Museum.)

In September 1959, the production and writing staff of the Texhoma *Times* newspaper pauses during their printing duties to pose for a group photograph. Today, only Hooker, Guymon, Beaver, and Oklahoma Panhandle State University in Goodwell print newspapers to share Panhandle news. (Courtesy Texhoma Historical Society and Museum.)

Pictured is the west side of Main Street in Goodwell in the 1920s. The same bank of buildings stands today and houses a bank, a tag agency, an insurance agency, an accounting firm, and a self-serve laundry. The street's opposite side has the community park, Hill Toppers Senior Citizen Center, and the post office. The business portion of Goodwell's main thoroughfare is just a block long. (Courtesy No Man's Land Museum.)

Owned by W.W. Grooms, Ross Oldaker, and Jim Prevett, the Goodwell Implement Company sold items for the home and machinery for farms and ranches. This photograph was taken in 1928, a few years before the business closed due to a decrease of farming operations during the Great Depression and the Dust Bowl, which hit the Oklahoma Panhandle particularly hard. (Courtesy No Man's Land Museum.)

The man second from the left, Frank Sewell, was the president of Goodwell's First National Bank in 1920. The other men in this photograph are, from left to right, J.J. Dimmitt, a local rancher; Arthur Littel, bank vice president; E. Lee Nichols, bank cashier; and Ed Isaacs, a county farmer. Oklahoma Panhandle State University named its administration building after Sewell to honor his support in establishing the institution in 1909. (Courtesy No Man's Land Museum.)

Volunteer firemen in Guymon, the county seat of Texas County, show off their new horse-drawn fire equipment in the early 20th century on a corner of Main Street. Today, Guymon maintains one of the best fire departments in Oklahoma and will soon build a second firehouse, as the community has grown large enough to support another station. (Courtesy Texhoma Historical Society and Museum.)

This Guymon building housed the First National Bank in 1909. Edward T. Guymon had a grocery store in Liberal, Kansas, and in the early 1890s, he bought land in Oklahoma hoping that the Rock Island Railroad would locate a stop there; it did. Originally called Sanford, the name changed to Guymon as people thought the name too similar to nearby Stratford, Texas. (Courtesy Texhoma Historical Society and Museum.)

Major-league sports have never made it to the Panhandle. However, this photograph proves that sports have long been important to the life of the region. This game is not quite at the major-league level, but it is baseball nonetheless. In the 1920s, women in Guymon put together two teams, found a couple of bats and a baseball or two, and had themselves a game. Spectators were not difficult to find. There is no record of the game's outcome. (Courtesy No Man's Land Museum.)

Nearly every community on the High Plains has its own cattle sale barn. Here, at the Guymon sale barn, ranchers sell and buy breeding and feeder stock for their cattle herds. Auctioneers call out for bids as the animals, aided by ring men, enter the sale ring on one side and exit on the other side to make way for more animals. (Courtesy Charla Lewis.)

Seaboard Farms became a major employer beginning in 1995 when it established this pork-packing plant in Guymon. The corporation raises, finishes, and slaughters its own hogs. Seaboard employs nearly 2,500 people, including many Hispanics. The influx of immigrants from Mexico and Latin America has greatly impacted the Panhandle and Guymon, in particular, especially in regard to education, economics, housing, health, and social services.

The Hispanic influence is great in the Panhandle. Most Spanish-speaking immigrants come from Mexico, but some hail from Guatemala, Honduras, and other Central American countries. They have come to work in area meat-packing industries, like Seaboard in Guymon; National Beef in Liberal, Kansas; and JBS in Cactus, Texas, since the early 1990s. Several immigrants have opened stores and restaurants in Guymon, boosting the Panhandle economy and making a diverse and colorful Main Street. Because of the increase in immigration, the population of Texas County increased 5.1 percent between 2000 and 2010. Texas County is the only Panhandle county to gain in population during that time span.

Hispanic culture is clearly evident in the Panhandle. Many communities, especially Guymon, host popular cultural celebrations and events attended by Hispanics and Anglos alike, such as the Fall Fiesta and the spring Cinco de Mayo event. Guymon High School and Oklahoma Panhandle State University (OPSU) in Goodwell have active Hispanic student dance troupes that keep busy performing at many venues in the Panhandle. These dancers represent the Corazon de OPSU dance troupe. Each summer, the troupe participates in the Mexican Traditions Camp, where dancers learn about Mexican culture and new *folklorica* dances. (Both courtesy Hector Cobos Leon.)

The Oklahoma Panhandle has many towns with unusual names, and Hooker is one of them. Hooker rests in Texas County, not far from the Kansas border. Other strangely named Panhandle towns include the now-abandoned Beer City, Beatrice, Gray, and Carrizo. Some communities have lost their vigor and size but still remain in a diminished form, such as Straight, Wheeless, Felt, and Slapout.

In the 1930s, unmarried men in Hooker were either proud of their marital status or wanted to advertise it when they created the Bachelors' Club. There is no report on the qualifications of membership, whether they had regular meetings, what their club constitution proposed, or if any of them ever married. (Courtesy ArVel White.)

All the fashionable ladies in Hooker went to Main Street to shop at White's Ladies Store, which specialized in millinery. The town's odd name came from the nickname of a local man named John Threlkeld, originally from Kentucky. He arrived as a working cowboy in 1873 and stayed in the area for 30 years. Friends called him "Hooker" because he could rope so well. The American Legion baseball team in Hooker is known as the Horny Toads, which only adds to the double entendre of the community's name. (Courtesy ArVel White.)

Beaver started life as Beaver City in the early 1880s, established at the halfway point on the Jones-Plummer Trail that connected Dodge City and a trading post in the Texas Panhandle. Frank Dale Healy took this photograph of Beaver's main street in 1886. Healy, a US deputy marshal and the sheriff of Beaver City, also manned the land office in Woodward, 82 miles southeast. (Courtesy Jones-Plummer Museum.)

In the early 1900s, Ben Kinder worked as the bartender at a saloon in Beaver City. The saloon displayed assorted odds and ends, bottles, and mirrors. As usual, a saloon provided an escape and entertainment for men, and most frontier communities had many of them. In northern Beaver County in the 1880s, Beer City had probably more saloons than any other Panhandle community ever did. (Courtesy Jones-Plummer Museum.)

Citizens inspect the ruins on the east side of Douglas Avenue in Beaver the morning after a fire destroyed the majority of the community on May 26, 1913. Ironically, early on in Beaver's history, people feared flooding from the Beaver River more than they feared fire. (Courtesy Jones-Plummer Museum.)

These men from the Beaver Boosters Club greet the first airplane to land in Beaver County. The pilot and passenger recline in front of the Boosters. In 1883, thirteen years after Beaver's start, its population had only increased to 112. By 1910, it had a population of 326. (Courtesy Jones-Plummer Museum.)

This general store was a main business in Knowles in Beaver County. It started out as Sands City in late 1906. However, when Sands City applied for a post office, its name somehow got changed to Knowles. Today, Knowles has evaporated. (Courtesy Jones-Plummer Museum.)

Here is a photograph of the main street of Forgan in 1912, the first year that train service entered the Panhandle. The Beaver County town got its name from a Chicago banker, James B. Forgan, who backed the railroad—the Wichita Falls and Northwestern. Appreciative Panhandlers honored his support by naming the new town after him. (Courtesy Jones-Plummer Museum.)

Founded in 1903, Floris in Beaver County sat halfway between Beaver and Liberal, Kansas. Gyrtrude and Byron Derthick staked a claim on 160 acres and established the community with this general store. They then applied for a post office, naming the settlement after their daughter. The store's second floor became the place to hold events in the town, hosting dances, meetings, and other communal gatherings. (Courtesy Jones-Plummer Museum.)

Slapout, in Beaver County, has a population of eight and one business—this convenience store, fuel stop, and garage. It got its name when the owner of the original store slapped the counter and told customers he was "slapout" of something he did not have. During the Depression, highway worker Tom Dawes erected a sign there that read as follows: "Slapout, Okla., Highway 270, Pop. 75, Speed limit: 90 mi. an hour, Fords, do your best."

In this photograph, T.L. Lemmons, the elderly man on the left, receives the 1976 Olympic torch during its run across the United States. Lemmons owned the Slapout Service Station. During the Great Depression, he sold fuel to people leaving the Panhandle for greener pastures. Not all could afford gasoline, so many of them sent Lemmons nickels, dimes, and quarters years later to repay him for his acts of kindness. (Courtesy Frank Lemmons.)

Four

SCHOOLS OF
THE PANHANDLE

The American West saw itself settled and tamed when bathtubs, curtains, churches, and schools came to town. The Oklahoma Panhandle was no different. Settlers built the towns, brought in their families, and educated themselves. Each Panhandle community had a school, and the number of country schools that once existed in the Panhandle is nearly impossible to tell, as they dotted the landscape about every five miles. Names of country schools like Gray, Blue Mound, Willowbar, Burton, and Clear Lake have faded even from history books, but teachers still teach Panhandle children in small schools such as Keyes, Felt, and Yarbrough. Some of these schools, such as Optima and Straight, have only pre-kindergarten through sixth-grade classes.

The Panhandle has a four-year college in Goodwell, Oklahoma Panhandle State University (OPSU). It began as an agricultural high school prep institution in 1909, and through the years, it has become a singular institution of higher education on the High Plains. OPSU is an obvious choice for Panhandle residents to attend, for it is quite distant from other universities in the five-state area. The closest college is West Texas A&M University in Canyon, Texas, some 130 miles away.

Panhandle residents value knowledge and realize that the future rests in what they can learn today. Education and the use of cutting-edge technology have always been important to the residents of the Oklahoma Panhandle, and they will continue to support educational opportunities.

Zilpha McClain French served as the second female county superintendent of schools in the state of Oklahoma. Here, she sits in her office in the Cimarron County Courthouse in Boise City in the second decade of the 20th century. A crack shot in her free time, she made her rounds of Cimarron County schools in one of the first automobiles in the county. Originally from Nebraska, she came to Oklahoma Territory in 1905 and homesteaded with her two sisters and brother. She died in 1951. (Courtesy Cimarron Heritage Center.)

As a schoolteacher in a one-room schoolhouse, Frank Neil (back row, fourth from the left) taught students of all ages at the Riverside Red School House in Beaver County. This photograph was taken during the 1897–1898 school year. Today, nothing remains of the site. (Courtesy Jones-Plummer Museum.)

Students at the Elmwood School District No. 25 in Beaver County pose with their teachers, Mr. Brown and Mattie Gregg (back row, fifth and sixth from the right, respectively), in 1906. There is no longer an Elmwood School. Elmwood, Oklahoma, sits on the top of a small hill south of Beaver and supports only one business, a convenience store. (Courtesy Jones-Plummer Museum.)

The coach and the Hooker High School football team in their uniforms pose for their school photograph in 1924. Today, some Panhandle high schools do not have enough athletes to play 11-man football, so they play 8-man ball if they field a team at all. There are few schools that serve students through all 13 years of public school in the Panhandle. The only places that do are Turpin, Beaver, Hooker, Goodwell, Guymon, Hardesty, Tyrone, Yarbrough, Keyes, and Felt, and some of those are not really towns in the strictest sense of the word. Texhoma offers elementary and secondary public education—in two different states—but all students graduate from the Oklahoma side. (Courtesy ArVel White.)

The 1909 boys' basketball team and the coach of Hooker High School pose for their school photograph. The Hooker High School girls' basketball team poses during the same season. Both teams had the same coach, which is not unusual even today in small schools. Basketball continues to be a very popular sport in Panhandle high schools, with rabid fans and dedicated players and coaches. Women's athletics, such as softball and basketball, have always been played in Panhandle high schools. (Both courtesy ArVel White.)

These young ladies of the pep club cheered the sports teams at Beaver High School in 1926. Sports did and do play an important role for students in Panhandle schools and their communities. The only drawback to Panhandle sports is the long distances that teams must travel to their opponents' courts, diamonds, or gridirons. Winter weather plays havoc with schedules, causing cancellations, postponements, and scheduling problems. (Courtesy Jones-Plummer Museum.)

The Goodwell school band strikes a pose in 1935. Goodwell in Texas County became a community in 1902 and the location for the establishment of the Pan-Handle Agricultural Institute, now Oklahoma Panhandle State University, in 1909. It got its name from the sweet and plentiful water in the community's well. (Courtesy No Man's Land Museum.)

These children enjoy recess at the stone Boise City elementary school in the early years of the 20th century. The Boise City High School began in these several wooden buildings pictured below after the number of school-aged children overflowed the original school in the early decades of the 20th century. Later, the community constructed a blond brick school. The Boise City School District is the largest in Oklahoma, with an area of 888 square miles, so many students travel great distances each day. (Both courtesy Cimarron Heritage Center.)

This school on Texhoma's Texas side once educated only Texhoma's Texas children from first to eighth grade; there was another school for Oklahoma children. The two schools played each other in sports and had a strong rivalry. The Texas school's mascot was the Blue Bulldog, and the Oklahoma school's mascot was the Red Devil. Built in 1913, this building now serves as the elementary school for the community. Texhoma sports teams still have the Red Devil as their mascot. The Texhoma school basketball team and its coach sported lots of stripes in 1931. In the last quarter of the 20th century, Texhoma football and basketball teams forged a strong reputation and are well supported by their community. (Both courtesy Texhoma Historical Society and Museum.)

This photograph, taken May 18, 1910, shows the laying of the cornerstone of the first building—Hesper Hall—on the campus of Oklahoma Panhandle State University in Goodwell. The date was auspicious, as Halley's Comet also appeared that day. The college started in 1909 as Pan-Handle Agricultural Institute, a high school prep institution with an emphasis in farming instruction. Through its 100-year history, the school has become a leader in higher education on the High Plains and is known for its championship collegiate rodeo team, computer science department, and agriculture school, among other distinctions. It maintains an enrollment of 1,200 students, offers both two-year and four-year degrees, and draws students primarily from the five-state area. Many students commute daily from as far away as Borger, Texas, or Liberal, Kansas. (Courtesy No Man's Land Museum.)

Hesper Hall, the first building at Pan-Handle Agricultural Institute, housed everything needed by an institute of higher education in 1909: a library, gymnasium, classrooms, an auditorium, and administrative offices. Hesper got its name from the Greek name for the evening star. The building was torn down to make way for a new Hesper in 1948. (Courtesy Panhandle State Association of Alumni and Friends.)

Hughes-Strong Hall has housed the school's music and theater programs since 1925, and its original white oak stage floor is still in excellent shape. It is now surrounded by other campus buildings and hosts many Panhandle cultural and entertainment events. Supposedly, three friendly female ghosts and a nice elderly gentleman wearing a cardigan haunt the building. (Courtesy Panhandle State Association of Alumni and Friends.)

Pictured are the first faculty members of Pan-Handle Agricultural Institute in the 1912–1913 school year. The institution's first president, S.W. "Daddy" Black, sits on the far right. These initial instructors shared their personal book collections to make the school's first library holdings, which were housed in one room of the first campus building, old Hesper Hall. Early on, the school was known as "rag town" because many male students lived in white canvas tents pitched on campus, for there were few dormitory spaces or local accommodations for them to rent. Initially, individual students assumed the responsibility of planting and tending a tree. That special care paid off, for today, the campus with its many trees is a welcome spot of respite and shade on an otherwise treeless plain. (Courtesy Panhandle State Association of Alumni and Friends.)

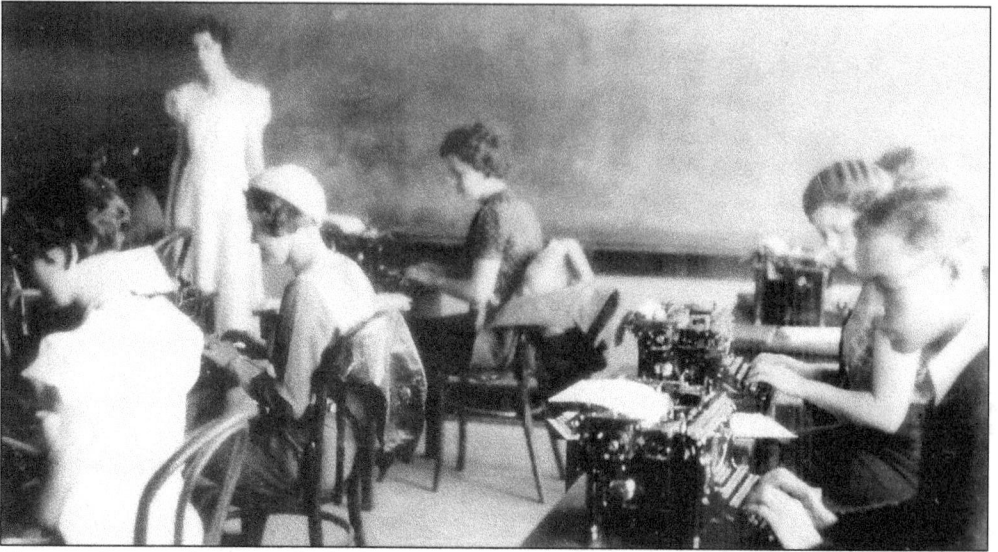

These students work in an early-day business class at Pan-Handle Agricultural Institute. Originally, the school offered secondary education for agriculture students. In 1921, the state legislature allowed the school to offer two-year college degrees and changed the name to Panhandle Agricultural and Mechanical College. Four years later, it offered baccalaureate degrees. The college became known as Oklahoma Panhandle State University in 1974. (Courtesy Panhandle State Association of Alumni and Friends.)

Students at Oklahoma Panhandle State University have long been able to learn the skills of the carpenter and woodworker in fabrication and construction classes. Industrial arts degrees remain popular. This class photograph from the 1930s shows well-dressed students planing away in a woodworking class. (Courtesy Panhandle Association of Alumni and Friends.)

Football became a college sport for the Pan-Handle Agricultural Institute in 1919. Athletes played early football games on a patch of land that at times grazed sheep. After World War II, men returning to college and desiring to play football leveled the field and cleared the weeds themselves. During the war, the gridiron had been used to grow wheat. (Courtesy Panhandle State Association of Alumni and Friends.)

Panhandle Agricultural and Mechanical College cheerleaders in the 1920s were known as the "Red Hots" and cheered all college athletic teams along the sidelines and court. The school mascot and team names have changed several times through the years, from the Tigers in early days to the Aggies of today. (Courtesy Panhandle State Association of Alumni and Friends.)

The *Sower* stands on the OPSU plaza in the center of campus. S.W. "Daddy" Black served as the first president of Pan-Handle Agricultural Institute, and he wanted a piece of artwork that would lend sophistication to the fledging campus. He contacted famed sculptor Frank Ingels in 1915 and asked for "something . . . that would inspire our young folks." Unfortunately, Black had no money in the school's budget to pay for such inspiration from such a noted artist. Therefore, Ingels, who had relatives in Texas County and knew of the school from them, donated the statue. It was officially dedicated in July 1915. Ingels is the sculptor who designed a similar bronze statue that sits atop the state capitol building in Lincoln, Nebraska. Some have thought that the *Sower* is a duplicate of the Lincoln statue, but this is inaccurate. (Courtesy Panhandle State Association of Alumni and Friends.)

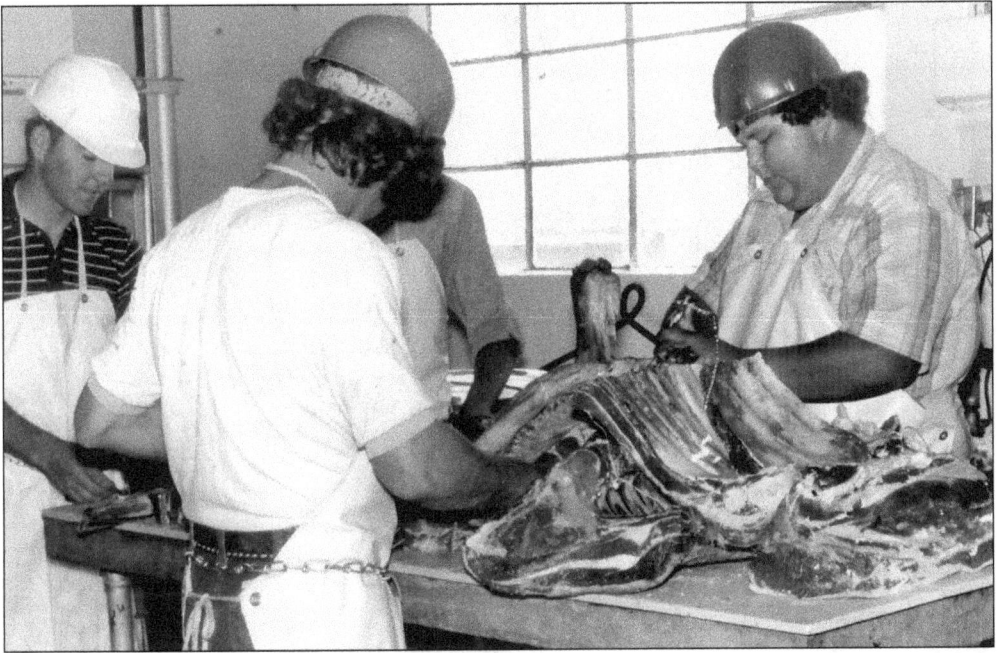

The Estes Firestone Meat Lab at Oklahoma Panhandle State University has two purposes. First, it serves as a laboratory for meat science students to learn the art of meat cutting for the retail market and to prepare students to work as meat inspectors. Second, it affords the local community a meat market where shoppers can buy cuts prepared by students. (Courtesy Panhandle State Association of Alumni and Friends.)

The Science and Agriculture Building is the newest building on campus, with state-of-the-art science labs and a greenhouse. It houses a water-quality testing lab, used frequently by Panhandle businesses and communities to test drinking water for contaminants. It is much easier to bring water samples to OPSU rather than to overnight samples to Oklahoma City, nearly 300 miles, for the same tests. Here, Nicole Crowley and Camron Nisly (right) learn about skeletal structure from Dr. Justin Collins.

The college livestock judging team has always been an integral part of the agriculture program at Oklahoma Panhandle State University and proves itself a capable competitor at national contests, where teams from major universities like the University of Louisville and Auburn University also compete. Livestock judges analyze farm animals like cattle, hogs, horses, and sheep according to the animals' form, fitness, and quality. Judges become experts in analyzing data and at public speaking, expressing their decisions and the reasons for these decisions very quickly. (Courtesy Panhandle State Association of Alumni and Friends.)

Pan-Handle Agricultural Institute offered agricultural training, so it needed a farm. In 1910, Oklahoma transferred the experiment station in Fort Supply to the school, and that entity became the farm. The institute's second president, J.F. Sharp, who served from 1915–1919, stands with the school's Herefords. The farm, now southeast of campus, rests on over 2,000 acres. (Courtesy Panhandle State Association of Alumni and Friends.)

In 1952, Panhandle Agricultural and Mechanical College and 14 area beef producers established the first beef bull performance-testing program in Oklahoma. It had a single goal—to improve beef cattle performance. Since then, OPSU has gathered data on 5,485 bulls. The bull test, the oldest running bull test in the nation, occurs each February. (Courtesy Panhandle State Association of Alumni and Friends.)

Practice makes perfect, so OPSU rodeo team members, such as Oney Martinez, practice often. The OPSU men's rodeo team has a storied past. Men's team members brought home four College National Finals Rodeo titles in 1997, 1998, 2000, and 2004. Between 2000 and 2010, OPSU cowboys and cowgirls won many individual national titles as well: Jordan Muncy Taton for breakaway roping and women's all-around in 2010, Krista Johnson for breakaway roping in 2008, Taos Muncy for saddle bronc in 2007 (the same year he won the world saddle bronc title at the National Finals Rodeo), Erica Brown for breakaway roping and Trell Etbauer for steer wrestling in 2005, Jett Hillman and Logan Olson for team roping in 2001, and Jesse Bail for men's all-around in 2000. It is not easy being a college rodeo competitor, for students must maintain their studies, provide their own transportation to other college rodeos, pay their own rodeo entry fees, and tend to their own horses. (Courtesy Panhandle State Association of Alumni and Friends.)

Weston Clark Taylor, a student at OPSU, participated in the steer wrestling event at the 2010 College National Finals Rodeo in Casper, Wyoming. Rich in cowboy and cowgirl legacy, OPSU has won four men's team National Finals titles since 1997. Taylor hails from Perryton, Texas. (Courtesy Laura Hays.)

Dr. Lynn Gardner, longtime OPSU rodeo coach and chemistry professor, stands in front of just a few of the trophies garnered by the university rodeo team in the 1980s. Students from the United States and Canada attend OPSU to participate on the nationally acclaimed rodeo team. (Courtesy Panhandle State Association of Alumni and Friends.)

People may believe that because of its location, OPSU would not attract foreign students, but that assumption is incorrect. International students make up approximately three percent of the university's enrollment, and as a result, OPSU hosts several annual events celebrating diversity. Students from places including Argentina, Poland, Nigeria, the Gambia, Canada, Brazil, and England have come to receive their baccalaureate degrees from OPSU.

The Oklahoma State Legislature dedicated a 20-mile stretch of Highway 54, from Texhoma to Guymon, as the Oklahoma Panhandle State University Centennial Corridor in honor of the university's 100th anniversary. This fall 2009 photograph features, from left to right (directly under the sign), Dr. Sara Jane Richter, Centennial Committee chair; Jill Olson holding Trighton Moore; Dr. Brent Burgess holding daughter Josephine; and Troy Morris, president of the Panhandle State Association of Alumni and Friends. (Courtesy Doris Looper.)

February 23, 2009, was Oklahoma Panhandle State University Day, honoring the university's centennial at the Oklahoma state capitol. Alumni, students, and faculty members shown here are, from left to right, Lloyd Looper, J.B. Flatt, David Miller, Sara Jane Richter, Tito Aznar, Representative Gus Blackwell, Carlee Scofield, Katie Wiggins, Doris Looper, and Brent Shoulders. (Courtesy Stuart Ostler.)

www.arcadiapublishing.com

Discover books about the town where you grew up, the cities where your friends and families live, the town where your parents met, or even that retirement spot you've been dreaming about. Our Web site provides history lovers with exclusive deals, advanced notification about new titles, e-mail alerts of author events, and much more.

MADE IN THE 🇺🇸**USA**

Arcadia Publishing, the leading local history publisher in the United States, is committed to making history accessible and meaningful through publishing books that celebrate and preserve the heritage of America's people and places. Consistent with our mission to preserve history on a local level, this book was printed in South Carolina on American-made paper and manufactured entirely in the United States.

This book carries the accredited Forest Stewardship Council (FSC) label and is printed on 100 percent FSC-certified paper. Products carrying the FSC label are independently certified to assure consumers that they come from forests that are managed to meet the social, economic, and ecological needs of present and future generations.

FSC
Mixed Sources
Product group from well-managed forests and other controlled sources

Cert no. SW-COC-001530
www.fsc.org
© 1996 Forest Stewardship Council

Find Your Place in History.

www.ingramcontent.com/pod-product-compliance
Lightning Source LLC
Chambersburg PA
CBHW050710110426
42813CB00007B/2142